The
UNITED
STATES
PRESIDENTS

John F. KENNEDY

Megan M. Gunderson

Big Buddy Books

An Imprint of Abdo Publishing
abdopublishing.com

abdopublishing.com

Published by Abdo Publishing, a division of ABDO, PO Box 398166, Minneapolis, Minnesota 55439.
Copyright © 2017 by Abdo Consulting Group, Inc. International copyrights reserved in all countries. No part of this book may be reproduced in any form without written permission from the publisher. Big Buddy Books™ is a trademark and logo of Abdo Publishing.

Printed in the United States of America, North Mankato, Minnesota
062016
092016

THIS BOOK CONTAINS
RECYCLED MATERIALS

Design: Sarah DeYoung, Mighty Media, Inc.
Production: Mighty Media, Inc.
Editor: Lauren Kukla
Cover Photograph: JFK Library/Museum
Interior Photographs: Alamy (p. 9); AP Images (pp. 5, 6, 7, 11, 15, 19); Getty Images (p. 29);
    JFK Library/Museum (pp. 7, 13, 17, 21, 23, 25, 27)

Cataloging-in-Publication Data

Names: Gunderson, Megan M., author.
Title: John F. Kennedy / by Megan M. Gunderson.
Description: Minneapolis, MN : Abdo Publishing, [2017] | Series: United States
    presidents | Includes bibliographical references and index.
Identifiers: LCCN 2015957498 | ISBN 9781680781052 (lib. bdg.) |
    ISBN 9781680775259 (ebook)
Subjects: LCSH: Kennedy, John F. (John Fitzgerald), 1917-1963--Juvenile
    literature. | Presidents--United States--Biography--Juvenile literature. |
    United States--Politics and government--1961-1963--Juvenile literature.
Classification: DDC 973.922/092 [B]--dc23
LC record available at http://lccn.loc.gov/2015957498

Contents

John F. Kennedy

John F. Kennedy was the thirty-fifth US president. He was the youngest man ever elected to the office.

Kennedy took office at a **challenging** time. America was fighting against **Communism**. This type of government was spreading throughout the world.

Sadly, President Kennedy never finished his first term. On November 22, 1963, he was murdered in Dallas, Texas. The world was saddened by the loss of this popular leader.

Timeline

1917

On May 29, John Fitzgerald Kennedy was born in Brookline, Massachusetts.

1952

Kennedy was elected to the US Senate.

1946

Kennedy was elected to the US House of **Representatives**.

1953

On September 12, Kennedy married Jacqueline Lee "Jackie" Bouvier.

1962

Kennedy handled the Cuban **missile** crisis.

1960

Kennedy was elected the thirty-fifth US president.

1963

Lee Harvey Oswald shot John F. Kennedy in Dallas, Texas, on November 22.

7

Young Jack

John Fitzgerald Kennedy was born on May 29, 1917, in Brookline, Massachusetts. His family called him Jack. His parents were Joseph Patrick Kennedy and Rose Fitzgerald Kennedy. Jack had eight brothers and sisters.

★ FAST FACTS ★

Born: May 29, 1917

Wife: Jacqueline Lee "Jackie" Bouvier (1929–1994)

Children: three

Political Party: Democrat

Age at Inauguration: 43

Years Served: 1961–1963

Vice President: Lyndon B. Johnson

Died: November 22, 1963, age 46

Jack spent his early years at this house in Brookline, which is near Boston, Massachusetts.

Jack went to schools in New York and Connecticut. In 1935, he finished his schooling. That summer, he studied **economics** in England.

Next, Jack entered Princeton University in New Jersey. However, he became sick and had to return home. In autumn 1936, Jack entered Harvard University in Massachusetts.

Jack's father became **ambassador** to Great Britain in 1937. So, the Kennedy family moved to London. Jack worked for his father during the summers.

★ DID YOU KNOW? ★

John F. Kennedy's grandfather served as the mayor of Boston, Massachusetts.

Jack (*left*) and his father (*center*) hoped his brother Joseph Jr. (*right*) would enter politics.

World War II Hero

In 1939, **World War II** began. In 1941, Kennedy joined the US Navy. He took command of a boat called the *PT-109*. But a Japanese ship sank the boat.

After the sinking, Kennedy and his crew swam three miles (5 km) to an island. Kennedy pulled a hurt man as he swam. He then secured his crew's rescue.

Sadly, Joseph Jr. died in the war. After his death, Kennedy became the family's **political** hope. He returned to Boston to prepare.

Kennedy earned a medal for the bravery and leadership he showed when his boat was attacked.

Congress

In 1946, Kennedy ran for a seat in the US House of **Representatives**. His family helped him campaign. Kennedy easily won the election.

Congressman Kennedy was in favor of low-cost housing. And, he also worked for higher wages. Kennedy also backed plans aimed to help stop the spread of **Communism**.

In 1952, Kennedy decided to run for the US Senate. Once again, his family helped him campaign. Kennedy won!

Kennedy's younger brother Robert (*right*) was his campaign manager in 1952.

Senator Kennedy helped pass several laws that were important to Massachusetts. He also worked to improve **civil rights**. Then, in 1953, Kennedy married Jacqueline Lee "Jackie" Bouvier.

In 1954 and 1955, Kennedy had operations on his back. While he rested, Kennedy wrote a book. It is about eight of the bravest US senators. The book came out in 1956.

Meanwhile, Kennedy was preparing for his next **political** steps. He was thinking about becoming president. He began by winning reelection to the US Senate seat in 1958. The win proved Kennedy's popularity.

The Kennedys had two children, Caroline and John Jr. A third son, Patrick, died as a baby.

The 1960 Election

In January 1960, Kennedy announced he was running for US president. The **Democratic** party backed him. The **Republicans** chose Richard Nixon to run.

That fall, Kennedy and Nixon met for a set of **debates**. For the first time in US history, the debates were shown on TV. Many Americans watched them. Viewers felt Kennedy had won.

The 1960 presidential election was one of the closest in US history. Still, Kennedy beat Nixon. He became the thirty-fifth US president.

Texas senator Lyndon B. Johnson (*right*) became Kennedy's vice president.

Making Plans

Kennedy became president on January 20, 1961. He had many plans when he took office. These included **programs** for higher wages and aid for the poor. He also hoped to improve **civil rights**.

During this time, America was part of the **Cold War** with the Soviet Union. Another plan was to put a person on the moon before the **Communist** Soviet Union did. As a result, Kennedy greatly improved the US space program.

John Glenn (*right*) was the first American to travel around Earth in a spacecraft.

21

Relationships with other countries were another concern for Kennedy. American officials wanted to stop the spread of **Communism**. So, they trained a group of Cubans to overthrow Cuba's Communist leader. In 1961, the group **invaded** Cuba at the Bay of Pigs. However, the effort failed.

Then, in 1962, Communist China invaded India. Kennedy sent weapons to India's army. Meanwhile, South Vietnam was fighting Communist North Vietnam. Kennedy sent thousands of US military advisers to help the South Vietnamese.

PRESIDENT KENNEDY'S CABINET

January 20, 1961–November 22, 1963

★ **STATE:** Dean Rusk

★ **TREASURY:** C. Douglas Dillon

★ **DEFENSE:** Robert S. McNamara

★ **ATTORNEY GENERAL:** Robert F. Kennedy

★ **INTERIOR:** Stewart L. Udall

★ **AGRICULTURE:** Orville L. Freeman

★ **COMMERCE:** Luther H. Hodges

★ **LABOR:** Arthur J. Goldberg,
   W. Willard Wirtz (from September 25, 1962)

★ **HEALTH, EDUCATION, AND WELFARE:**
   Abraham A. Ribicoff,
   Anthony J. Celebrezze (from July 31, 1962)

In October 1962, Kennedy learned **nuclear missile** bases were being built in Cuba. He wanted to stop Soviet ships from bringing supplies there. So, Kennedy stated that the US Navy would block Cuba's coast.

The Soviet leader said his country would guard its shipping rights. A nuclear war could begin. But Kennedy held his ground.

The Soviet ships stayed away from the blocked area. Kennedy won the showdown! This event became known as the Cuban missile crisis.

★ SUPREME COURT ★
APPOINTMENTS

Byron R. White: 1962

Arthur J. Goldberg: 1962

Soon after the Cuban missile crisis, the United States, Great Britain, and the Soviet Union signed an agreement limiting nuclear weapons testing.

Trouble in Dallas

In 1963, Kennedy prepared for reelection. On November 22, he and Jackie flew to Dallas, Texas. They then traveled through Dallas in a car with the top down.

At about 12:30 pm, Kennedy was shot in the head and the throat. Just 30 minutes later, he died. Vice President Johnson became president.

Lee Harvey Oswald was soon arrested for killing Kennedy. However, Oswald said it was not him. Two days later, a man shot and killed Oswald.

President and
Mrs. Kennedy
arrived in
Dallas on the
presidential
airplane,
Air Force One.

The entire world was shocked by Kennedy's death. Leaders from 92 countries came to pay their respects. Kennedy was buried near Washington, DC.

As president, John F. Kennedy faced **challenges** around the world and at home. He gave America a goal for future space travel. But, Kennedy is best remembered for leading the country through the Cuban **missile** crisis.

★ DID YOU KNOW? ★

After Kennedy's death, several buildings were created or renamed in his honor, including John F. Kennedy International Airport in New York.

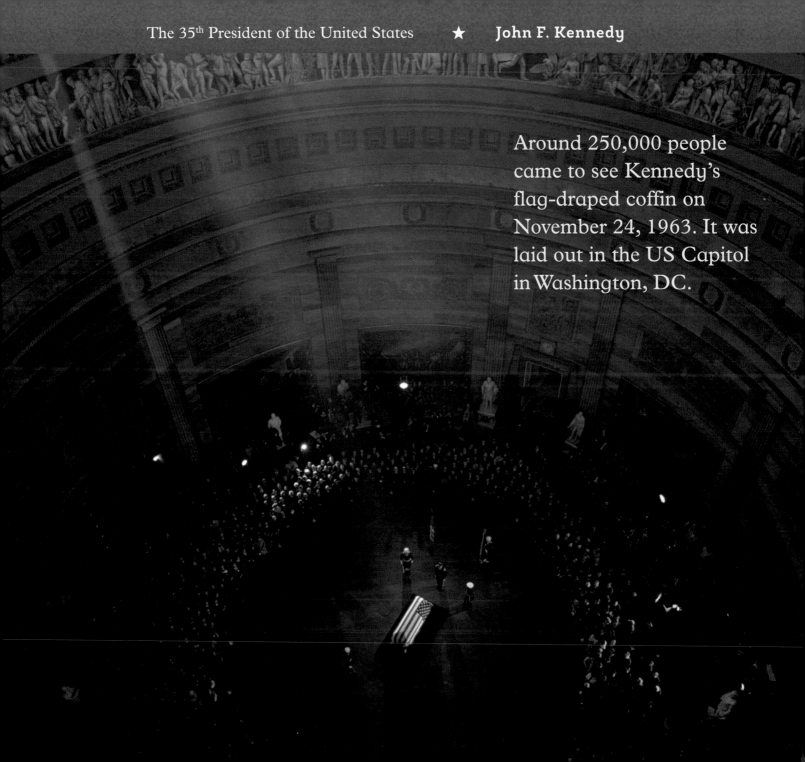

Around 250,000 people came to see Kennedy's flag-draped coffin on November 24, 1963. It was laid out in the US Capitol in Washington, DC.

Office of the President

Branches of Government

The US government has three branches. They are the executive, legislative, and judicial branches. Each branch has some power over the others. This is called a system of checks and balances.

★ **Executive Branch**

The executive branch enforces laws. It is made up of the president, the vice president, and the president's cabinet. The president represents the United States around the world. He or she also signs bills into law and leads the military.

★ **Legislative Branch**

The legislative branch makes laws, maintains the military, and regulates trade. It also has the power to declare war. This branch includes the Senate and the House of Representatives. Together, these two houses form Congress.

★ **Judicial Branch**

The judicial branch interprets laws. It is made up of district courts, courts of appeals, and the Supreme Court. District courts try cases. Sometimes people disagree with a trial's outcome. Then he or she may appeal. If a court of appeals supports the ruling, a person may appeal to the Supreme Court.

Qualifications for Office

To be president, a candidate must be at least 35 years old. The person must be a natural-born US citizen. He or she must also have lived in the United States for at least 14 years.

Electoral College

The US presidential election is an indirect election. Voters from each state choose electors. These electors represent their state in the Electoral College. Each elector has one electoral vote. Electors cast their vote for the candidate with the highest number of votes from people in their state. A candidate must receive the majority of Electoral College votes to win.

Term of Office

Each president may be elected to two four-year terms. The presidential election is held on the Tuesday after the first Monday in November. The president is sworn in on January 20 of the following year. At that time, he or she takes the oath of office.
It states:

> I do solemnly swear (or affirm) that I will faithfully execute the office of President of the United States, and will to the best of my ability, preserve, protect and defend the Constitution of the United States.

31

Line of Succession

The Presidential Succession Act of 1947 states who becomes president if the president cannot serve. The vice president is first in the line. Next are the Speaker of the House and the President Pro Tempore of the Senate. It may happen that none of these individuals is able to serve. Then the office falls to the president's cabinet members. They would take office in the order in which each department was created:

Secretary of State

Secretary of the Treasury

Secretary of Defense

Attorney General

Secretary of the Interior

Secretary of Agriculture

Secretary of Commerce

Secretary of Labor

Secretary of Health and Human Services

Secretary of Housing and Urban Development

Secretary of Transportation

Secretary of Energy

Secretary of Education

Secretary of Veterans Affairs

Secretary of Homeland Security

Benefits

★ While in office, the president receives a salary. It is $400,000 per year. He or she lives in the White House. The president also has 24-hour Secret Service protection.

★ The president may travel on a Boeing 747 jet. This special jet is called Air Force One. It can hold 70 passengers. It has kitchens, a dining room, sleeping areas, and more. Air Force One can fly halfway around the world before needing to refuel. It can even refuel in flight!

★ When the president travels by car, he or she uses Cadillac One. It is a Cadillac Deville that has been modified. The car has heavy armor and communications systems. The president may even take Cadillac One along when visiting other countries.

★ The president also travels on a helicopter. It is called Marine One. It may also be taken along when the president visits other countries.

★ Sometimes the president needs to get away with family and friends. Camp David is the official presidential retreat. It is located in Maryland. The US Navy maintains the retreat. The US Marine Corps keeps it secure. The camp offers swimming, tennis, golf, and hiking.

★ When the president leaves office, he or she receives lifetime Secret Service protection. He or she also receives a yearly pension of $203,700. The former president also receives money for office space, supplies, and staff.

PRESIDENTS AND THEIR TERMS

PRESIDENT	PARTY	TOOK OFFICE	LEFT OFFICE	TERMS SERVED	VICE PRESIDENT
George Washington	None	April 30, 1789	March 4, 1797	Two	John Adams
John Adams	Federalist	March 4, 1797	March 4, 1801	One	Thomas Jefferson
Thomas Jefferson	Democratic-Republican	March 4, 1801	March 4, 1809	Two	Aaron Burr, George Clinton
James Madison	Democratic-Republican	March 4, 1809	March 4, 1817	Two	George Clinton, Elbridge Gerry
James Monroe	Democratic-Republican	March 4, 1817	March 4, 1825	Two	Daniel D. Tompkins
John Quincy Adams	Democratic-Republican	March 4, 1825	March 4, 1829	One	John C. Calhoun
Andrew Jackson	Democrat	March 4, 1829	March 4, 1837	Two	John C. Calhoun, Martin Van Buren
Martin Van Buren	Democrat	March 4, 1837	March 4, 1841	One	Richard M. Johnson
William H. Harrison	Whig	March 4, 1841	April 4, 1841	Died During First Term	John Tyler
John Tyler	Whig	April 6, 1841	March 4, 1845	Completed Harrison's Term	Office Vacant
James K. Polk	Democrat	March 4, 1845	March 4, 1849	One	George M. Dallas
Zachary Taylor	Whig	March 5, 1849	July 9, 1850	Died During First Term	Millard Fillmore

PRESIDENT	PARTY	TOOK OFFICE	LEFT OFFICE	TERMS SERVED	VICE PRESIDENT
Millard Fillmore	Whig	July 10, 1850	March 4, 1853	Completed Taylor's Term	Office Vacant
Franklin Pierce	Democrat	March 4, 1853	March 4, 1857	One	William R.D. King
James Buchanan	Democrat	March 4, 1857	March 4, 1861	One	John C. Breckinridge
Abraham Lincoln	Republican	March 4, 1861	April 15, 1865	Served One Term, Died During Second Term	Hannibal Hamlin, Andrew Johnson
Andrew Johnson	Democrat	April 15, 1865	March 4, 1869	Completed Lincoln's Second Term	Office Vacant
Ulysses S. Grant	Republican	March 4, 1869	March 4, 1877	Two	Schuyler Colfax, Henry Wilson
Rutherford B. Hayes	Republican	March 3, 1877	March 4, 1881	One	William A. Wheeler
James A. Garfield	Republican	March 4, 1881	September 19, 1881	Died During First Term	Chester Arthur
Chester Arthur	Republican	September 20, 1881	March 4, 1885	Completed Garfield's Term	Office Vacant
Grover Cleveland	Democrat	March 4, 1885	March 4, 1889	One	Thomas A. Hendricks
Benjamin Harrison	Republican	March 4, 1889	March 4, 1893	One	Levi P. Morton
Grover Cleveland	Democrat	March 4, 1893	March 4, 1897	One	Adlai E. Stevenson
William McKinley	Republican	March 4, 1897	September 14, 1901	Served One Term, Died During Second Term	Garret A. Hobart, Theodore Roosevelt

PRESIDENT	PARTY	TOOK OFFICE	LEFT OFFICE	TERMS SERVED	VICE PRESIDENT
Theodore Roosevelt	Republican	September 14, 1901	March 4, 1909	Completed McKinley's Second Term, Served One Term	Office Vacant, Charles Fairbanks
William Taft	Republican	March 4, 1909	March 4, 1913	One	James S. Sherman
Woodrow Wilson	Democrat	March 4, 1913	March 4, 1921	Two	Thomas R. Marshall
Warren G. Harding	Republican	March 4, 1921	August 2, 1923	Died During First Term	Calvin Coolidge
Calvin Coolidge	Republican	August 3, 1923	March 4, 1929	Completed Harding's Term, Served One Term	Office Vacant, Charles Dawes
Herbert Hoover	Republican	March 4, 1929	March 4, 1933	One	Charles Curtis
Franklin D. Roosevelt	Democrat	March 4, 1933	April 12, 1945	Served Three Terms, Died During Fourth Term	John Nance Garner, Henry A. Wallace, Harry S. Truman
Harry S. Truman	Democrat	April 12, 1945	January 20, 1953	Completed Roosevelt's Fourth Term, Served One Term	Office Vacant, Alben Barkley
Dwight D. Eisenhower	Republican	January 20, 1953	January 20, 1961	Two	Richard Nixon
John F. Kennedy	Democrat	January 20, 1961	November 22, 1963	Died During First Term	Lyndon B. Johnson
Lyndon B. Johnson	Democrat	November 22, 1963	January 20, 1969	Completed Kennedy's Term, Served One Term	Office Vacant, Hubert H. Humphrey
Richard Nixon	Republican	January 20, 1969	August 9, 1974	Completed First Term, Resigned During Second Term	Spiro T. Agnew, Gerald Ford

PRESIDENT	PARTY	TOOK OFFICE	LEFT OFFICE	TERMS SERVED	VICE PRESIDENT
Gerald Ford	Republican	August 9, 1974	January 20, 1977	Completed Nixon's Second Term	Nelson A. Rockefeller
Jimmy Carter	Democrat	January 20, 1977	January 20, 1981	One	Walter Mondale
Ronald Reagan	Republican	January 20, 1981	January 20, 1989	Two	George H.W. Bush
George H.W. Bush	Republican	January 20, 1989	January 20, 1993	One	Dan Quayle
Bill Clinton	Democrat	January 20, 1993	January 20, 2001	Two	Al Gore
George W. Bush	Republican	January 20, 2001	January 20, 2009	Two	Dick Cheney
Barack Obama	Democrat	January 20, 2009	January 20, 2017	Two	Joe Biden

"Ask not what your country can do for you—
ask what you can do for your country." John F. Kennedy

★ WRITE TO THE PRESIDENT ★

You may write to the president at:
The White House
1600 Pennsylvania Avenue NW
Washington, DC 20500

You may e-mail the president at:
comments@whitehouse.gov

37

Glossary

ambassador—the job of speaking for, or representing, one country to other countries.

challenge (CHA-luhnj)—something that tests one's strengths or abilities.

civil rights—the rights of a citizen, such as the right to vote or freedom of speech.

Cold War—a period of conflict between the United States and its allies and the Soviet Union and its allies after World War II.

Communism (KAHM-yuh-nih-zuhm)—a form of government in which all or most land and goods are owned by the state. They are then divided among the people based on need.

debate—a planned discussion or argument about a question or topic, often held in public.

Democratic—relating to the Democratic political party. Democrats believe in social change and strong government.

economics—the science of the way in which goods and services are produced, bought, and sold.

invade—to send armed forces into a place, usually to try to take it over.

missile—a weapon that is thrown or fired to hit a target.

nuclear—a type of energy that uses atoms. Atoms are tiny particles that make up matter.

politics—the art or science of government. Something referring to politics is political. A person who is active in politics is a politician.

program—a plan for doing something.

relationship—the way people feel about or act toward one another.

representative—someone chosen in an election to act or speak for the people who voted for him or her.

Republican—a member of the Republican political party.

World War II—a war fought in Europe, Asia, and Africa from 1939 to 1945.

★ WEBSITES ★

To learn more about the US Presidents, visit **booklinks.abdopublishing.com**. These links are routinely monitored and updated to provide the most current information available.

Index